I0803569

The Monarch Butterfly

LEVEL 8

/ch/y/

DECODABLES BY jump!

Teaching Tips

Purple Level 8

This book focuses on the phonemes **/ch/y/**.

Before Reading

- Discuss the title. Ask readers what they think the book will be about. Have them support their answer.
- Discuss the book's focused phonemes. Explain that each can have different sounds. /Ch/ can have a /tch/, /sh/, or /k/ sound. /Y/ can have a /y/, long /e/, long /i/, or short /i/ sound. Give examples of each.

Read the Book

- Encourage readers to read independently, either aloud or silently to themselves.
- Prompt readers to break down unfamiliar words into units of sound and string the sounds together to form the words. Then, ask them to look for context clues to see if they can figure out what these words mean. Discuss new vocabulary to confirm meaning.
- Urge readers to point out when each focused phonics phoneme appears in the text. What sound does it make?

After Reading

- Ask readers comprehension questions about the book. What are the stages of a monarch butterfly's life?
- Encourage readers to think of other words with the /ch/ or /y/ phoneme. On a separate sheet of paper, have them write the words into columns by sound.

5357 Penn Avenue South
Minneapolis, MN 55419
www.jumplibrary.com

Library of Congress Cataloging-in-Publication Data is available at www.loc.gov or upon request from the publisher.

ISBN: 979-8-88996-900-6 (hardcover)
ISBN: 979-8-88996-901-3 (paperback)
ISBN: 979-8-88996-902-0 (ebook)

Photo Credits

Images are courtesy of Shutterstock.com. With thanks to Getty Images, Thinkstock Photo and iStock photo. Cover – ilikestudio. 3 – irin-k, Andrey Pavlov, Protasov AN. 4–5 – Georgi Baird, Rabbitti. 6–7 – Breck P. Kent, Sari ONeal. 8–9 – Agnieszka Bacal, ItsAngela. 10–11 – Darkdiamond67, Leena Robinson. 12–13 – Leena Robinson, Martin Leber. 14–15 – Atosan, JHVEPhoto. 16 – Shutterstock.

Can you name these insects?

There are many different types of butterflies. One of these pretty insects is the monarch butterfly, which is easy to spot thanks to its bright wings.

You can tell if a butterfly is a monarch by checking the patterns on its wings. Monarchs have symmetrical wings with matching black lines and white patches.

Symmetrical means that one side is exactly the same as the other side but flipped.

Monarchs do not have wings their whole lives. A monarch starts life as a tiny egg attached to a leaf. A female monarch butterfly lays one egg at a time.

Monarch eggs hatch a few days after they are laid. They begin as little caterpillars and start eating the plant they hatched on.

Caterpillars need to eat a lot before they can mature into their butterfly form. They spend a few weeks eating constantly and shedding their skin to get bigger.

Monarch caterpillars eat lots of milkweed. This plant has toxic chemicals in it that lots of animals cannot eat. By eating milkweed, caterpillars stop predators from eating them!

To change into a butterfly, a caterpillar attaches to a plant and turns into a chrysalis. This is a case a caterpillar stays in while its wings grow.

A monarch butterfly cannot fly right after it comes out of its chrysalis. It must wait for its damp wings to dry.

Monarchs do not grow bigger after the chrysalis phase, but they do still have to drink nectar for energy. They get nectar from flowers.

Monarch drinking from an orchid

Nectar is liquid, so monarchs suck it up with a straw-like mouthpart called a proboscis. They mostly taste with their feet, which means they can taste a flower as soon as they land.

When it gets chilly in fall, some monarchs in North America migrate to a warmer place. Huge numbers of them travel to exactly the same spot in Mexico.

The trip to Mexico is a bit of a mystery to insect experts. Each butterfly that migrates there has never been there before but knows where to go!

Say the name of each object below. Is the "y" in each a /y/, long /e/, long /i/, or short /i/ sound?

yo-yo

bunny

fly

gymnast

FIRST ROUTINES

MORNING ROUTINE

by Jenna Lee Gleisner

TABLE OF CONTENTS

tadpole books

WORDS TO KNOW

bed

breakfast

brushes

eat

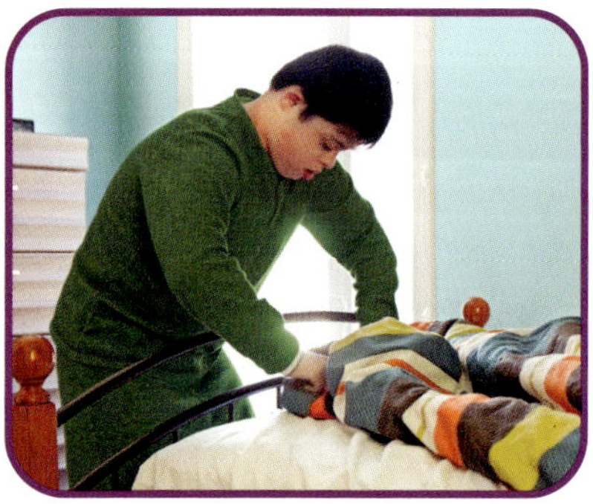

makes

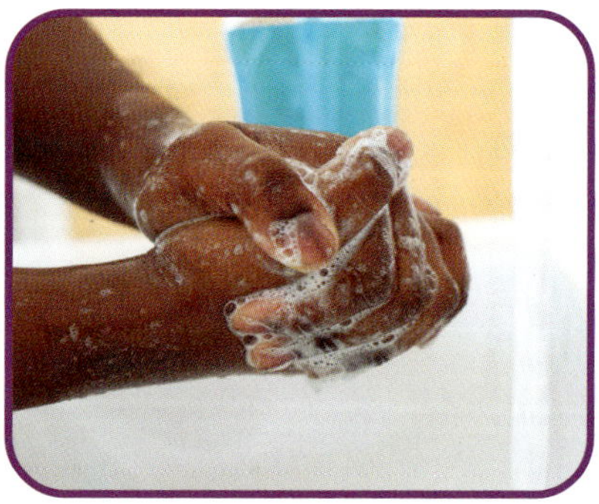

washes